BEING UNMISTAKABLY
CHRISTIAN AT WORK

BEING UNMISTAKABLY CHRISTIAN AT WORK

Don Latham

Terra Nova Publications

Terra Nova Publications International Ltd
PO Box 2400, Bradford on Avon, Wiltshire BA15 2YN

Registered Office (not for trade):
21 St Thomas Street, Bristol BS1 6JS

ISBN 1 90194 940 0

Printed in Great Britain
by Bookmarque Ltd, Croydon

CONTENTS

1

BEING UNMISTAKABLY CHRISTIAN AT WORK

It was my first meeting as a non-executive Director of the Health Authority.

"Mr Latham, I hear you're religious," said the medical consultant.

"It's not true, but these rumours do get spread!" I replied. "I'm a Christian: how did you happen to hear about that?"

"Well, the Chief Executive bought a copy of your book in Tesco, and said we all have to read it." What an encouraging start that was, as I began my new appointment!

As NHS directors, our work included going out on hospital visits together. One day we were doing some ward visiting when a beautiful black nurse threw her arms around me and kissed me! I leave to your imagination the astonishment of some of my female colleagues who were visiting with me. You should have seen their faces when she then called me "brother". I let them go on wondering about this as we continued to walk around the wards. Later I told them what it was all about. She was my Christian 'sister', whom I had met at a Christian conference where I was leading a parish weekend.

It should come naturally to us to be distinctive Christians in the workplace. The workplace is a platform for Christian witness. I have seen many of my colleagues come to know Jesus. This can happen for you, too. The areas we need to consider are: our calling from God; our attitude to work; our stewardship; our time management; how we handle ourselves in a personal way; ethical behaviour; wisdom; spiritual life – and how we maintain that life in the workplace; exercising spiritual gifts at work;

and witness. Work, and exercising our Christian faith at our place of work, is a most exciting dimension of our Christian life.

2

CALLING

Your work is your calling. It is not a secondary calling in comparison with being a pastor. If you are called, you are anointed and equipped for your job. The order of priorities is that after God, and your relationship with Him, and then your family, comes work. Then comes other Christian activity. Your work is an integral part of your Christian activity. It is vitally important to realise that your work is your calling. I have prayed for a number of people who had never previously had prayer for their calling in the workplace. Do ask other Christians to pray with you for your calling and for God's anointing on your work.

When you know that God has called you to your career, then you can know that He is your partner in it. It is He who calls, anoints and equips you. Whatever your calling, whether it is in industry, commerce, craft or profession, you are not on your own. Remember that God is your partner in the workplace; you can show confidence in Him to handle all the problems you face.

People will look at you when you are in the place of pressure, and they will be observing how you cope with it. Do you panic? Or do you show a quiet, calm assurance? What does your secretary (if you have one) observe when seeing you, a Christian, facing pressure? Do you show confidence in God to deal with the problems? Do you show maturity in the workplace? When change comes, how do you react? Do you embrace it, seeing it as an opportunity to allow God to do a new thing in your life? Or do you respond as people usually do in the natural —with fear? Change always creates tension, because it brings uncertainty. Do you resent change? Is your normal reaction to argue for the status quo? People will look at you as a Christian and see whether you show maturity.

Are you consistent? Do your colleagues see you, all week long, full of joy, wanting to do your best? Interestingly, during my time as a local authority Chief Executive, the Christians were very often the ones who were picked out and commented upon as being excellent at what they did. Frequently, this happened: my Councillors would identify people doing an exceptionally good job, displaying a good attitude. And if Christians were not doing their best, I drew it to their attention. I belonged to the same family as them, and I expected all members of the family to behave well and to give of their best. I want our Christian family to have a good reputation. To be consistent is vital. Don't try to talk about your faith unless you are consistent. Or your colleagues might fear becoming like you!

3

ATTITUDE

Isn't it wonderful how positive Christians can be? Never negative; never critical; always looking for the best in others....

It is so important to be positive. Your Christian witness will be useless if you are a moaner. Remember that there will be no moaning and grumbling in the Kingdom of Heaven! Our God is a positive God. We, too, need to be positive —particularly in what we say. Our words can be creative and powerful.

We can change the whole atmosphere of the work situation by what we speak. People are sometimes healed by being set free from negative words they have spoken. Recently I prayed for a man with crippling arthritis who had spoken negative words over himself. He had a compassionate intention, but the words were spoken foolishly. We broke the power of those words, in the name of Jesus. He was completely healed by the Lord.

Try to look for the good in situations, and avoid speaking negatively. The positive will then drive out the negative. In church life we concentrate far too much on what is negative. The antidote is to concentrate on the positive.

Go for excellence, and always give of your best. This does not mean being mistake-free, but you will learn from your mistakes. You cannot expect to be distinctively Christian and an effective witness without a real willingness to do your best.

God has given us great potential in Him. We need to fulfil this by being creative. If we ask God for His creative ability to be released in us —He will do it! I remember praying for someone at a conference, when God told me that He would give him a creative idea that would make him successful, and would bring a lot of money, through him, into God's Kingdom. He did! God gave him that creative idea. God is the God of invention and creativity. Ask God to give you creativity in your place of work.

Exercise mutual respect for people: equality, without political correctness. Having worked in local government, I believe in equality. As Christians, we should demonstrate this. For example, I found that women had not been promoted to senior positions, and was able to promote them. Respect for others is essential. Do not expect your witness to be effective if your attitude to others is not right: it will be observed.

Learn from mistakes and try again. Our mistakes are opportunities to learn. To British Christians, Peter is the guy who sank; to the Americans he walked on water —even though he got his feet wet. I prefer the American view of this! I have done things which involved stepping out of the boat. We have to be prepared to take some risks.

4

STEWARDSHIP

Exercise good stewardship. People will look at how we order our lives.

Have clear priorities. The Parato principle, from management science, says that 20% of your activity will produce 80% of the results. I concentrate on that 20% which produces the maximum results. Many of us spend 80% of our life producing 20% of the possible results! People have asked how, as a Chief Executive, I managed to do so much in my life.

I ask God to show me what the key things are which are going to lead to success and help me to be effective. They are very basic things: praying; spending time with Him. This is vitally important for people in church leadership too. They are called upon to do all sorts of things, but then do not have time to do the thing that really counts in terms of making oneself effective.

Ask God to show you what the key activities are. When I used to start work on a Monday, I would ask Him to do this for me. Getting to the office early (7 a.m.), I would begin with prayer. Working in the public sector, I prayed for those in the private sector —that they might get to work soon, to earn the money to pay for us! I said in my prayer: 'Father, what are the things to tackle this week —the key tasks? If there are any unpleasant ones that I need to carry out, then show me.'

There were rarely more than six vital things. Write down what you hear from Him, and declare that you are now going to tackle them.

People who achieve things, and are excellent in what they do, have clear priorities. So be organized and not confused. Any spirit of confusion needs to be dealt with. It may just be a matter of having some basic training in throwing things away. If you are disorganized, don't feel guilty: just do something about it. A big pile of paper around the workplace can just show that you are out of control. Our God doesn't want us to be overwhelmed by situations, but in control of what we are doing. Delegate work, and use your time effectively.

This is something that is vital in the life of the church. Frequently, there are too few people trying to do too many things. We need to learn the art of delegation, involving and empowering other people —not just 'passing the buck', but sharing the work out with them. I love managing teams, in which, often, the team members are more skilled than I am in most areas. It is good to get others for whom we are responsible to work creatively together, in order to achieve results.

When I was in my first senior management job, as an Assistant Director of Social Services, I was trying to merge three departments, doing three years' work in three months. I thought that by working day and night I could do it. I couldn't. Then God took me away on a senior management course for ten weeks. It was meant to be very intensive, but I found it, by comparison, relaxing! God taught me about people —that they are gifted and can do things. I learnt to start delegating. When I returned to the office after the course, I called together all my senior managers and said, "OK, spend the day talking about me. How do I need to operate differently as your manager, to be effective?" Quite a challenging day.

They returned and told me. They said, "We want to spend more time with you. We want you to visit us. We want to do a lot of the work you are doing. We want to do it for you."

It changed my whole style. This is something which needs to happen in the life of the church. We have so many passengers in the church, who have never been involved.

Develop your talents and use them to the full. God expects this of us. If you are in a position where this is not happening at the moment, then pray that God will put you in the place where you can use and develop those gifts. You are intended by God to enjoy your work.

5

TIME MANAGEMENT

One of the most precious things that God has given us is time. The thing that will mark out the Christian is a good attitude toward time management. I find that to schedule time and set deadlines is helpful. One day I looked at my diary and saw that I had thirty talks to give over the next few months, at the same time as working pretty intensively. As I thought about this, God sent me to Bermuda for a week! Taking my laptop computer, I worked on the plane. Then I rose at four o'clock each morning and did four hours work to catch up, joining Hilary for breakfast at eight o'clock. A hurricane came one day. That really allowed me to get up to date!

Set yourself deadlines. If you don't, then things just mount up. I find I am creative when I have a deadline to meet. Do you find that you always put off the most difficult task until you have to do it? Then you do it and think, 'If only I had done this before, I wouldn't have to worry about it.' Tackle large tasks in chunks. It may seem that a job is so big, you think, 'How am I going to do it?' You can't eat an elephant in one bite; you can take a bite at a time. If a big issue arises and you think you have to resolve it immediately, God will show you how to deal with it, a bite at a time, gradually working through it.

Conserve time. Make time for yourself. I like people. As a Chief Executive, I had an open door policy, relating to people —which, as a 'people-person', I enjoy. But, in order to do quality things as a Christian, you need to set and arrange times that are going to be undisturbed, when you can think. There had to be some times when I would be unavailable to others. As an early riser, I used to love the two hours before most of the staff arrived. That was my thinking time; my prayer time; my 'getting ready for the day' time —the time for doing what I wanted to do before I was available to other people, to help them to do what they needed to do. The trouble was that by the time I left, after five years in the post, many of the staff were coming in at eight o'clock —because they wanted to be there! There was no pressure to do this; they just did not want to miss out on what was happening. Do remember to make time for yourself —this is so important. In the busy lifestyle we have as Christians, we must make sure we set aside the time to reflect, to relax, and to do the things we need to do.

Make the most of meetings. Have you attended many frustrating meetings? Those who sit on some Parochial Church Councils may identify with this. There are meetings when you reflect: 'We could have got through the business, positively, in half the time actually taken; the meeting has been badly chaired; the agenda has not been put together properly; it hasn't been clearly focused. We would have been better off staying at home.'

I like meetings, because I have seen very creative things happen in them. So often, though, we fail to make the best use of the time. It matters how you set up meetings and use them. Let your meetings be structured, and make good use of the time spent in them.

Use your journey times effectively. In that way we can double the effective use of time. Travelling by car can include listening to taped material. Rail travel can be an ideal time for reading. If you want to make space for yourself on a train, just take out your Bible! It will either draw you into a fantastic conversation, or you will find you have acquired some personal space!

Christians should be examples of how to make the best use of time. If you are always overloaded, you are doing too much.

6

PERSONAL LIFE

Influence by example. We should be a compassionate people, concerned for others. It is so often the small things you do that will mark you out. What do you do when a work colleague's eighteen-year-old son is killed in a car accident? Most people avoid the colleague because they don't know what to say. I remember writing and just simply saying, 'We can't imagine what you are going through. We want you to know we are praying for you.'

A few weeks later, the colleague came to my office and knocked on the door. He said, "Mr Latham, thank you for the letter, it meant so much to us."

We should be compassionate in the workplace. We all go through difficult situations, and many people don't know how to relate to such things. We need to give an example.

We should give recognition to others. There is nothing more positive than giving affirmation. People give of their best for those who do this. I worked for one manager who only spoke to me if there was something wrong. We never really developed a relationship. Giving recognition is so important: it is one of the most motivating things you can do. And it doesn't cost you anything, financially. So often, people gave me that sort of affirmation on the final day, when I was leaving a post. They would say, 'Don, we are so sad you are leaving. You've made such a contribution here.' And I thought: 'Why didn't someone tell me this before? I wouldn't be going." Rubbing salt into the wound, they might add: 'We had such great ideas for your future career.'

Do you affirm staff? Do you say, when

appropriate, 'This is an excellent piece of work'? Letters came in, sometimes, congratulating our authority for doing some work well. I would go personally, as Chief Executive, and give a copy of that letter to the individual responsible, saying, 'I want to thank you personally for the excellent job you are doing, on behalf of the community.' If it was the man who sweeps the streets in Bradford-on-Avon (a town within my District), I would go there and park next to the man with the brush and say, 'Fred, thank you. Here's a letter from a member of the public, saying what a great job you are doing.' Affirmation is of key importance. As Christians we should be positive people, affirming our colleagues in what they are doing.

Do not seek personal advantage. You may need to sacrifice for colleagues. If you are always the one who has to be top of the pile, it does affect your witness. God doesn't put us where we are to be trampled over, but having the right attitude sometimes means holding back and giving for colleagues. People will see that.

Show joy. We do have to be spiritual in the workplace. There is only one fruit of the Spirit, with different components —joy is part of it. You cannot be both spiritual and miserable at the same time! The joy of the Lord is your strength. People will look at you when you are going through tough times. They will be aware that you are a Christian, and observe the quality of your life. What will mark you out is that joy in the Lord. Are we manifesting the fruit of the Spirit in the workplace? A key issue for a Christian at work is praying for colleagues and the place of work. Are you doing this? As we start to pray for them, those with whom we work will come to know Jesus. Situations will change. Prayer does it. I don't see people coming to know Jesus without someone having prayed. It may be a parent, a family member or a neighbour. I want to have witnessed to all those with whom I work, and want there to be nothing in my life that hinders them from coming to Christ. I don't want people to be able to say, 'Don, it was great to work with you, but you never told me what motivated you in life.'

7

ETHICAL STANDARDS

People will know that we are Christians, and observe what we do. We are not to be conformed to this world. People should see in us something distinctive. Sometimes the gospel causes offence, but in ourselves we are meant to be salt and light. Admittedly, it is easier if you are the boss, because you establish the corporate culture. There was no blasphemy when I was around. It is much more difficult if you are a contemporary or peer group member.

I know, having worked my way through those situations. But don't mind being different!

Be honest. In use of the employer's assets, even in small things, just be beyond criticism. In my payment for private telephone calls for the office – and I did not make many – I think I paid in more than anyone. When a time came that my employers tried to move me out of a job, because they decided they didn't want me, the first thing they spent the evening doing was going through my travel claims, trying to find some justification for my removal. Of course there was nothing. Personally, I didn't claim any subsistence, I paid for my own food. If I entertained guests, I paid for them myself. I wanted to be beyond question in all that I did. Don't you? On things like expenses, as Christians we need to be impeccable. Forget having effective witness if you are like everyone else —just stretching things to the limit.

Stand up to unethical, immoral pressures, injustice and unfair discrimination. Such things are found in the workplace, and it can be tough to be in these situations. I know what it is like to put my job on the line to stand up for what I believe to be right. There was no doubt,

I just had to do it. God put me in the situation. I understand the pressure that comes when making a stand like this.

Ask God for wisdom and it will be given to you. This is another key matter. It is tempting to think, 'I'll try to sort this out myself, and if I can't do so, then I'll ask God for the answer.' But you can ask God for wisdom before you even start to tackle the problem. If necessary, you may have to 'blow the whistle', not that Christians need always or automatically do so, for sometimes it is possible to deal with unethical situations without causing a furore.

God's wisdom is 'wise dominion'. He wants to put us in the place where we can exercise our godly authority under Him. We can bring that godly authority into our place of work or business. Wisdom is the possession of experience and knowledge, together with the power of applying them. Something should mark us out as Christians in the workplace, and this is an aspect of it.

One afternoon I was in a meeting at which a very complex personnel issue was being discussed. I was due to speak later on, at a meeting in Halifax, and I began to think, 'The way they are going on about this, I'll never get to Halifax. I won't just miss the dinner, I'll hardly be able to arrive in time to give my talk.' So I prayed. I was the only one in the room who was not a Chief Officer. It was a very serious matter under discussion, concerning a senior member of staff. As I prayed to God for wisdom, suddenly in my thoughts He dictated a letter to me. It just came to me so clearly. I coughed, and said to the Chief Executive, "Would you mind if I shared an idea?" ('Shared' —an absolute giveaway that I was a Christian!) The Chairman invited me to go ahead, and I dictated the letter back.

"Latham," said the Chairman of the Council, "that's brilliant."

For the next twenty minutes, others tried to think of better ideas. No-one could think of a better approach. They accepted the suggestion, and the complex personnel matter was resolved. When I left the Council, I was thanked for the wisdom God had given me in helping the Council. I had prayed for it.

There are two elements to wisdom. The Greek *sophia* means insight into the true meaning of things. God will tell you, a Christian, the hidden agenda. Often, sitting at a meeting, you know they are not discussing the real issue. This is not only true of board meetings, but also of church meetings. Often one thinks, as people talk: 'What is the real agenda here?' If you ask God for wisdom, He will give you insight about what is really going on. The second element, *phronesis*, is the ability to design modes of action with a view to the end result. Christians should be demonstrating God's wisdom.

God has put us in a place of work. It is our calling, our anointing; so we ask God for wisdom there. When we do pray for wisdom, ideas start to come —though not always immediately. I sometimes think, 'How shall I resolve this one?' Then I pray: 'Now Father, you know I need the resolution by tomorrow.' I might wake up late at night or in the morning, and suddenly it comes to me. The great thing is that what we are given is the word of God. If we are to be men and women who are walking in God's wisdom, we have to give the word of God priority in our lives. Sometimes people tell me they have been told to do various things, when I know they have not, because I have read the Book! God will never speak contrary to His word. The word of God must rise up in us by His Spirit. The word can be so amazingly accurate in its relevance to the work situation.

8

SPIRITUAL LIFE

We need to maintain our spiritual life. Make time for prayer. Pray in the Spirit; pray with the understanding. Paul says, "Pray in all kinds of prayers." I enjoy a busy lifestyle and hard work. But you have got to make time for prayer. Are you really praying about your place of work?

Arriving at work in the early morning, I would pray. Walking round the office, before the staff came to work, I would speak the presence of God, the Spirit of God, into the building. I prayed that people would want to come and work there; that they would want to succeed with me, working together; that it would be a good place to work; that there would be harmony, unity, creativity. We need to do this. I prayed for my colleagues. I prayed that in me, and in other Christian brothers and sisters on the staff – individually and corporately – they would see a reflection of Jesus; that they would see something that might attract them to him. I prayed for my secretaries, that they would come to know him. Sometimes, I must admit, I did not have the courage to go to Christian meetings which they nonetheless went to, and where they had a fantastic time with God. It all happens because you pray. If you are too busy to pray, then you are too busy. It is vital to maintain your faith. We need to hear the word of God; we need to read the word of God; we need to meditate the word of God. My wife and I love the word of God. Train and aeroplane journeys are excellent opportunities for extra Bible reading.

We need to exercise our faith. Ask God to give you opportunities to exercise faith as a

Christian. If you do that today, He will! Plan recreation times with your family. Plan quality time with them. You can have all the success you like, but if your family life falls apart, it is not success. We would take our children out for restaurant meals often, because they loved dining out. They still want to come on holiday with us, even though they are now married! I spoke over our children that they would be our best friends, because our children are a gift from God. I refused to speak that the teenage years would be problem years. I thanked God for the fact that they were different; that His hand was on their life; that He would cause them to succeed —in the right way, knowing Him, and His blessing.

In my experience, whenever I put my wife and children first, God promoted me. Whenever I gave God my ambition and my career and said, 'Hilary and my children mean more to me than those things', often within a few days the next job had been advertised, no removal of our home was necessary, and I knew that, despite the competition, yet again my five 'O' levels would beat a hundred or more graduates.

Avoid being the victim of 'gradualism'. When

we are working with groups that are pre-
dominantly composed of non-Christians, the
danger is that you can gradually become like
them. I had listened to some Christians in the
workplace who sounded no different from non-
Christians. They were saying exactly the same
things. One of my favourite Bible teachers,
Trevor Partridge, used the illustration of a frog.
If you put a frog in hot water, it will jump out.
If you put a frog into cold water and boil it up,
it will sit there until it gets boiled to death.
Sometimes we Christians are like that in the
workplace. We are in a minority and we begin
to take on the ethos and style, the attitudes
and language of those around us: then we have
lost our distinctiveness. It is not easy. It is a
challenge, like the whole of the Christian life.

9

SPIRITUAL GIFTS

I have already mentioned the need to speak God's blessing over your job and your place of work —because we seek the best, for His glory. If you are speaking doubt, fear, unbelief and problems over your place of work, that is what you will have —and you deserve it! For you are the person who can change the spiritual atmosphere in your workplace. You are a son or daughter of God, and you can start to speak God's word into the place. If you don't, then things will get worse. Expect to move in gifts of revelation, power and utterance. The gifts of the Spirit are for the workplace. People sometimes say, 'Don, I am so restricted at church; I can't use my spiritual gifts there.' I ask them, 'How long do you spend in church?' 'An hour and a half, on a Sunday,' comes the reply. I say, 'The good news is that for twenty two and a half hours on Sunday, you can be wildly free. During the week, there is no limitation. You can go for it. Isn't that exciting?'

I have seen the gifts of the Spirit operate in the workplace. God will give you words to speak. God's people should be speaking positively into the lives of other people. It should come naturally from us.

We can be prophetic in the workplace. Are you speaking positively about the future? Are you prophetic about your business plan? God told me to draw up a new business plan this year, to lay hands on it —and He would give me the plan. I did that a few years ago and He fulfilled exactly what He told me I would earn in my first year of working independently.

Many of us are involved in planning at work. God will give us the plans we need. We should pray for creativity, and for help in counselling other people. As managers, we should be the best, in terms of exercising such counselling skills as are appropriate to the manager's job.

10

WITNESS

Now we come to the heart of the matter. Unless we have right the things I have already written about, this section does not work! If we have understood and are applying the teaching already given, then this part will work easily.

Honesty, personal integrity and reliability are all integral to effective witness. People will look at the style of our lives before they listen to what we say. They have the right to do so. They will look at the good deeds that we do.

They will see if we are different. We have to show that to others —not in the kind of way that says, 'Aren't I good?' But people should see that, as Christians, there is something different that we have in our lives. We need to exercise spiritual gifts and be ready to share our faith as God prepares the way and provides the opportunity. Personally, I do not seek to make opportunities.

Are you looking for opportunities to minister to the non-Christians around you? We are to look and pray for revival. I long to see what we hear about in other nations, where huge numbers are queuing up for church! I long to see people turning back to God in the hundreds, not only the ones and twos. I met a businessman from Guatemala. He spoke of 95,000 people coming to know Jesus in one week in his country. That was through the witness of people in the workplace —not through evangelists.

Exercising spiritual gifts can come quite naturally. I wait for the opportunities to come, and then really go for them. We need to be set free from 'English reserve'. It happened for me one Sunday afternoon, when I let the vicar pray for me. You have to be desperate to go to the vicar on a Sunday afternoon —I was! I had been on many courses on witnessing; I had even taught on them. Have you ever tried to teach something when you cannot do it yourself? I thought I had been a 'good Christian' at work, but it was only after hands had been laid on me and I had a new experience of the Holy Spirit, following eighteen years of hyperactive Christianity, that I found witnessing became spontaneous and natural. Then God set me up, teaching me how to walk in faith at work.

An employee who worked for me had been depressed for a long time. A Christian doctor friend rang me and asked, "Don, is there anything you can do for her?"

I replied, "I don't normally handle personnel matters myself, but let's pray. If it is right, let's ask God to intervene."

We prayed on the telephone. The next day, my Chief Admin. Officer came to me. He said, "Don, is there anything you can do for Freda?" (Not her real name.) I rang her and asked if she would like to come and see me, so I could talk about the future. She agreed. I took an afternoon's holiday at home. (You never try to impose your faith, especially using your employer's time. I put in more time than I was ever paid for, but you have to be impeccable in these matters.) Because Freda was a woman, I had my wife with me.

Freda arrived. We talked about her future. After an hour I was feeling depressed! Then I asked, "Can I talk to you as a friend now, rather than as a boss, because I know the answer to your problems?" She gave me her permission. So then I talked to her about Jesus: the one who came to give his life for her, to forgive her, to give her new life, to set her free; to fill her with the power of God's Spirit. I sent her away with a copy of *The Happiest People on Earth* (an ideal book for depressed people!) and a copy of Mark's Gospel. I said, "Come back if you want to make the decision." She came back a few days later and sat down. I explained that it was a complete transaction: you give your total life to God and He gives everything He has to you. So I gave her a few moments to ponder this. She was ready. She gave her life to Jesus Christ. I prayed that she would be forgiven, born again of God's Spirit, set free from her depression, and filled with the Holy Spirit. The truth is that she could not move out of the chair for a couple of hours, as she sat there and the love and healing power of God just flowed through her.

My wife and I had coffee. It was two hours later that Freda felt fit to drive home. She phoned up three days later to say, "I want you to know, I'm a new person. I went to bed, then slept without the pills for the first time in months. I woke up in the morning and the 'dark tunnel' had disappeared." She was back at the office the following Monday.

She was the first. There were many to follow, as God started to train me. The next one was in a lift. A colleague got into the lift. He had had painful operations. I said to him, "How are things?"

He replied, "Don, I have these pains in my stomach. I have a ringing noise in my head from the time I wake up until the time I go to sleep." I felt compassion. If we are to be witnesses, it must flow from compassion. Do you want to hear the Holy Spirit speak to you? He will —with compassion. When I had received that power within me which raised Jesus from the dead, I said, "Jesus, I want to be able to release this power the way you did, to touch the lives of other people. How do I get it out?"

Jesus answered, "It is faith and compassion." And as I had compassion in the lift, the Holy Spirit said to me, "Pray for him; he is going to be healed." I did the fatal thing: I paused. As I went up to the next floor, something said to me, 'He is a subordinate of yours: you can't pray for him.' At the next floor, the thought came, 'What if nothing happens?' Have you heard that sort of voice?

Getting out of the lift, I thought of how I had wasted the God-given opportunity. He went to his office and I went to mine. I prayed, saying, "Father, I blew that. If you want me to pray, bring him to my room." I felt a sense of relief. I thought nothing would happen. Less than five minutes later, there was a knock on the door.

Taking a deep breath, I said, "Come in." In he came, and we discussed some financial issues concerning his job. Much later, he told me that when he had gone from the lift to his room, something told him that he had to make up a financial problem to come and discuss with me. What prayer will do....

When we had discussed the problem, then I needed to have faith. I said, "I believe that God wants me to pray for you. He is going to heal you." Not being a Christian, he didn't know God couldn't do it! I spent much of my time praying for non-Christians. If we do not do it, our colleagues will continue to go to so-called 'faith healers'; they may try alternatives, some of which are based on Eastern mysticism, and pay the price spiritually for that, without realising it. I am ready to pray, not as a faith healer but as a Christian —because I know that God responds to our prayers.

He agreed. I went round to the other side of the desk and laid hands on him, praying in the Spirit. The door to my secretary's office was open and I saw her there. She went on working at the computer, as though we did this every day of the week. He thanked me and returned to work. Some time later, I saw him, and he said, "Don, from the day you prayed for me, that noise (tinnitus) diminished day by day, and has now gone completely."

Even when I had an opportunity to move on in my career, sometimes fear held me back (and often we are robbed by fear). Waiting times are a preparation for the next thing. In one such time I read my Bible through at least twice a year, and I studied it, taking all the opportunities God gave me to witness to people. One lunchtime, in a meeting at work, we saw more than twenty come to know Jesus. We had invited a woman speaker who had a dynamic testimony. Two colleagues for whom I had been praying – but had not had the courage to invite – came without needing an invitation from me. I had thought the meeting quite inappropriate for them, yet they were both among those who gave their lives to Jesus.

I am not ashamed of Jesus. Are you? I want people to think well of me, but we are part of a 'royal family'. As a Christian I want to demonstrate that we have life in balance, but in such a way that it will attract people to Jesus. Whilst I do not force opportunities myself, if they are there I am ready to go for them. We can all think of the chances we have missed. God is so keen for people to come into His Kingdom that He is willing to use you continuously.

We need to ask God for boldness. The power of the Holy Spirit was given on the day of Pentecost to make the disciples bold witnesses. This is a prayer I can guarantee God will answer, because this is what Pentecost was all about. Once we visited Rome and saw the

Colosseum. I looked down and thought, 'Some of my Christian brothers and sisters of the early church gave their lives there —not because it was a 'good idea'; not because it was something that might have worked out. They were sure.' I want that boldness, in love, to be able to share Jesus with people.

People would say to me, 'Don, I wish I had your faith', and I would take them out for a meal. One of the first things that happened when I became Chief Executive was that I preached at a local church. Some of the staff, hearing about this, came to hear their new boss. One woman member of staff gave her life to the Lord on that first occasion. Some time later she came to the office with a seriously ill baby. Imagine a member of your staff bringing a baby to you for prayer.

Our Christian witness should be spontaneous and natural. One Monday my secretary, who had been a great support to me, was behaving strangely towards me. I had been there since 7 a.m. It was now 6.20 p.m. and she would normally have left for home some time earlier. I thought something significant was about to happen. Then, standing in my office, she looked at me and said, "Mr Latham, I became like you yesterday." I asked what had happened. She replied, "I went to church and heard about Jesus for the first time. I have given my life to him."

A few months later, I was speaking at a celebration service held at a theatre. Some members of my staff came, including my secretary. At the end of the evening she stood for prayer and she would not let anyone else pray for her. She said, "I'm not going to leave this place until you pray for me."

I had said to my staff, "You can never be dishonest on my behalf. You can't say, 'He's not available' when I am." So I had to see council taxpayers who insisted on seeing the Chief Executive. That led to some most significant meetings with people.

I will never forget one occasion when a man had booked an appointment for 3.40 p.m. one afternoon. He came into my office and sat down, saying, "Mr Latham, my business is in trouble. I can't continue for much longer, but I have a Christian who works for me. For the last two years he has sustained me in my business. He has refused a pay increase for that time. He has prayed for me. I said to him that I can't keep going. What shall I do? He said, 'Don't worry, I have booked an appointment for you to see the Chief Executive.'"

I carefully explained to him that the answer to his problem was Jesus, and said, "Are you ready? It means giving your whole life to Jesus. You give him your life, he'll give you his life. He'll forgive you, but it demands everything."

He replied, "Yes, please." Five minutes later he was born again, filled with the Holy Spirit and staggered out of my office as though we had been at the Members' drinks cabinet.

I do not try to impose my faith on others, but we should expect to have opportunities. People will look both at you and at those who are against you. I have experienced that, and had to speak God's blessings over those who were against me. Sometimes you hear accusations that are unjust. People will see how you respond to that. But we must be ready to lead others to Jesus Christ.

It was important in the most senior positions not to appear to favour unfairly those who shared my Christian faith. Pray for your employees. Pray for your employers, too. Many political leaders and members in the council were Christians. In a politically diverse council we had a corporate plan that was endorsed by all the councillors. My colleagues could not understand how I did that. It was by prayer and careful negotiation. I said to the councillors, "We will achieve far more by agreeing together what we do —if, over four years, we can agree an agenda that we will deliver to the community."

Ask God who you should pray for. At a seminar I met an ordinary working man who saw eight hundred of his work colleagues come to know Jesus. When we asked him how it had happened, he described how, when he had become a Christian, he started to pray for one of his work colleagues. Then he approached him and talked to him about Jesus. He gave his life to Jesus.

They started to meet together before the morning shift and pray for the next work colleague. Over a short period they saw the eight hundred men come to know Jesus in this way. Sadly, the local churches found it very difficult to deal with this and integrate the new converts. They could hardly believe what had happened. The local workplace church was bigger than all the other churches put together!

We need to pray, asking God to release His gifts in us so that we can be witnesses. The place for using spiritual gifting spontaneously and naturally is in the workplace. I was at my desk one day when a pain came in my back. That is often how I receive words of knowledge. I thought, 'If there is someone to pray for, show me who.'

Five minutes later a senior colleague came in. He said, "Don, I've just put my back out. I am in such pain." At such moments you have to speak.

I said, "I believe God is going to touch your back and heal it for His glory." Nothing happened that day.

The next morning he could not wait to come and see me. "What happened?" I asked nonchalantly.

He told me, "I thought about what you said all afternoon. Then I went back home and was lying on the bed, still in agony. We were due to fly to Australia and I said to my wife, 'You know Don Latham said God was going to heal my back for His glory?' Then there was a loud click in the bedroom. It was so loud we both heard it. My back was completely healed."

I replied, "The God who healed your back yesterday is the God who loves you and is going to Australia with you."

This should be ordinary witnessing. People tend not to forget such things. Sometimes you are forced into witnessing by your colleagues —even non-Christians. Some staff members came in, saying to me, "A secretary is sick in hospital: the doctors can't find out what's wrong with her. Will you go and pray?" At first, I declined. I did not know her, though we had spoken. I did not want to go. They – the non-Christians – insisted. So in the end, I relented. It was Parochial Church Council night. I turned up at the hospital in Bath on a wet Wednesday night. I prayed that she would be on her own, so she wouldn't be embarrassed. Opening the door in the hospital, I found she had three people with her. She looked up at me, and I could see from her face she was wondering, 'What is he doing here?' So I went in, discussed Bath rugby, the fact the weather was not too good.... Then I ran out of conversation. They were looking at me —her boyfriend and her parents.

I said, "I believe God wants me to pray for you; that He wants to heal you. Are you happy for me to pray?" The parents and boyfriend knelt on the hard floor, by the bed. I held her hands and prayed the most inept prayer for healing I have ever prayed, before or since. Then I said, "Goodnight. I've got to go; it's the PCC night." Later, I blanked the incident from my mind as we got embroiled in the exciting business of the church council. Within a few days she was healed.

So do not limit the way God will use you. He may not use you that way. There was a time when I would say to God, 'I don't want to be used that way. I want to do the works of Jesus, without healing. I know Jesus did a lot of it, and he said that the works he did would also be done by those who believe in him, but can I do that without healing, because I am an accountant?' The answer, of course, is that you have to do what God wants you to do in your life. If you work with normal colleagues you will often find that they are getting involved in occult and other things without realising what they are doing. We have the answer: Jesus. What I long to see is what is happening in so many other countries —especially, as I have seen for myself, in places such as Argentina —where Christian witness is so effective; where people are so in love with Jesus. We need the life of Jesus to be so evident in us *in our workplace* that we will get natural opportunities to witness for him.

WITNESS AND WORK
Brian Allenby
National Director, Christians@Work
ISBN 1901949281 £7.99
Encouragement to go on witnessing.
Includes helpful application of biblical themes.

WITNESS AND WORK RESOURCES
Brian Allenby
ISBN 1901949303 £7.99
Useful suggestions and guidance
for Christian fellowship groups.

CHAMPIONS FOR GOD AT WORK
David Kellett
ISBN 190194915X £8.99
A comprehensive biblical guide to faith
and workplace issues.